THE EARTH'S OCEANS

Composition and Underwater Features

Interactive Science Grade 8 |
Children's Oceanography Books

BABY PROFESSOR
EDUCATION KIDS

First Edition, 2019

Published in the United States by Speedy Publishing LLC, 40 E Main Street, Newark, Delaware 19711 USA.

© 2019 Baby Professor Books, an imprint of Speedy Publishing LLC

Baby Professor Books are available at special discounts when purchased in bulk for industrial and sales-promotional use. For details contact our Special Sales Team at Speedy Publishing LLC, 40 E Main Street, Newark, Delaware 19711 USA. Telephone (888) 248-4521 Fax: (210) 519-4043. www.speedybookstore.com

10 9 8 7 6 * 5 4 3 2 1

Print Edition: 9781541949676
Digital Edition: 9781541951471

See the world in pictures. Build your knowledge in style.
https://www.speedypublishing.com/

Contents

UNDERWATER FEATURES
OF THE EARTH'S OCEANS

In this book, we're going to talk about the composition and underwater features of the Earth's oceans, so let's get right to it!

Is It One Ocean or Four Oceans?

Our planet is named Earth, but the ironic thing is that most of the Earth's surface isn't covered by land at all. Over 70% of the surface of our planet is covered with water. Geographers call these bodies of water oceans.

OVER 70% OF EARTH'S SURFACE
IS COVERED WITH WATER

THE CONTINENTS SEPARATE THESE
OCEANS FROM EACH OTHER

The landmasses on Earth, called continents, separate these oceans from each other. However, if you look closely at a globe you will see that they all flow into each other. For that reason, sometimes they are thought of as one enormous global ocean.

If you think of the oceans as separate, then the Pacific Ocean is the largest. The Atlantic Ocean is the second largest in size, but it only has 50% of the volume of the Pacific. The Indian Ocean is third in size. It is surrounded by Africa, India, southeast Asia, and Australia. The Southern Ocean surrounds the continent of Antarctica and extends to the latitude of 60 degrees south. The Arctic Ocean is the smallest of all five. It encircles the North Pole and its surface is largely ice.

How Did the Oceans on Earth Form?

AT THE START, VOLCANOES COVERED
THE SURFACE OF THE EARTH

The Earth is about 4.54 billion years old. At the start, it was a rocky mass that was way too hot for oceans to form. Volcanoes covered the surface and spewed out ash, hot dust, and gases, which included water vapor. Over a very long period of time, these gases started to create Earth's atmosphere.

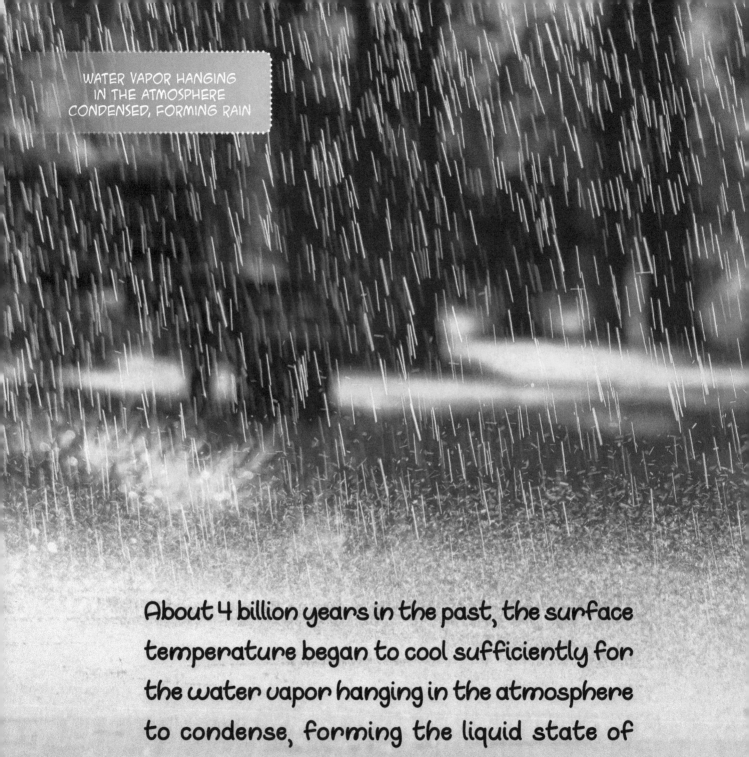

WATER VAPOR HANGING
IN THE ATMOSPHERE
CONDENSED, FORMING RAIN

About 4 billion years in the past, the surface
temperature began to cool sufficiently for
the water vapor hanging in the atmosphere
to condense, forming the liquid state of

water that we know as rain. The rain began to fill up the lower elevations on the surface of the Earth and eventually the oceans formed.

How Have the Earth's Oceans Changed Over Time?

The continents haven't always been where they are located today. About 245 million years ago, they were all joined into one large continent that today we call Pangea. Throughout Earth's history there have been several supercontinents and more than likely millions of years from now a supercontinent will form again. The continents move because the tectonic plates on Earth's surface shift due to volcanic activity.

PANGEA

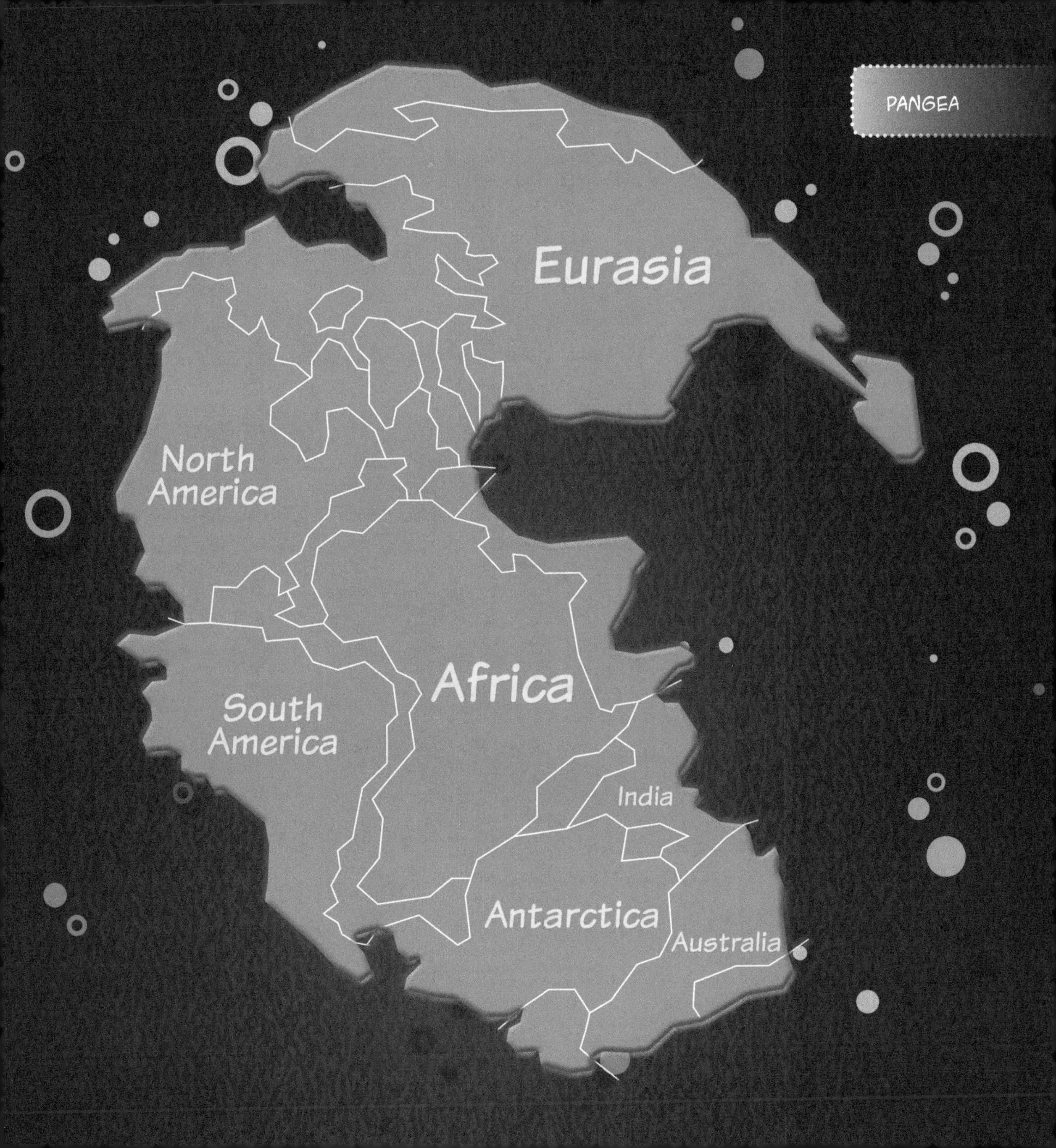
Eurasia
North America
Africa
South America
India
Antarctica
Australia

THE COAST OF ATLANTIC OCEAN
IN CANARY ISLANDS, SPAIN

About 180 million years in the past, Pangea began to break apart forming the northern section of what is now the Atlantic Ocean and also shaping the Indian Ocean. Most of the Atlantic Ocean was formed about 65 million years in the past. However, the southern portion of the Atlantic was much less wide at that time than it is now. The continents are shifting even today. They move extremely slowly however, only about 1 to 10 centimeters every year. The Pacific Ocean is starting to shrink, but some of the other oceans are increasing in size.

Why is the Water in the Oceans Salty?

We can't use ocean water for drinking because it's too salty for us. There are some animals that have special glands that remove salt, which makes it possible for them to drink salt water.

SEA TURTLES RID THEMSELVES OF EXCESS SALT THROUGH A "SALT GLAND" NEAR EACH EYE, MAKING THEM APPEAR TO BE CRYING

Most ocean salt is the same type that we use to flavor our food. The chemical formula for it is NaCL. The Na stands for Sodium and the CL stands for chloride. In addition to salt, the water in our oceans has other dissolved solids too, such as calcium, magnesium, sulfur, and potassium.

MOST OCEAN SALT IS THE SAME TYPE THAT WE USE TO FLAVOR OUR FOOD

AN AERIAL VIEW OF A FRESHWATER
RIVER MEETING THE SEA

Rivers and streams are freshwater sources. As their currents flow into the oceans, they wear away minerals from soil and rocks. Then, they carry these minerals, which have now been dissolved, into the ocean. So, you may be wondering if the water gets so salty and has all these dissolved minerals how does it ever go back to the form of fresh water again?

The ocean water evaporates due to heat. When it evaporates, it goes into the atmosphere as water vapor. When the water evaporates it leaves behind the heavier minerals that it contained. Then, when it rains or comes down as other forms of precipitation, it's fresh water.

Water Cycle

Deposition
Snow and Ice

Transportation
Wind and Atmospheric Pressure

SUN

Precipitation
Rain, Snow, Fog, Hail

Snowmelt

Condensation
Clouds and Fog

Transpiration
From Trees and Plants

Surface Flow

LAKE

Percolation
Subsurface flow

River Discharge

Evaporation
Liquid to Gas

Infiltration

OCEAN

OCEAN WATER EVAPORATES DUE TO HEAT

What is the Measurement of Salinity?

If you took a kilogram of salt water and heated it so it would evaporate completely, there would be about 35 grams of dissolved solids left over. That measurement, 35 grams per kilogram, is the measurement of the salinity of the salt water.

The salinity of ocean water isn't the same everywhere. For example, in the Middle East, the Red Sea has a high level of salinity due to the fact that the climate there is so hot. The hot temperatures cause a fast rate of evaporation, which leaves more salt as a residue.

RED SEA COASTLINE IN THE NATIONAL PARK OF RAS MUHAMMAD, EGYPT

Fresh water from streams and rivers flows into the ocean at the coastlines. In these areas, the salinity of the ocean water is less than average because so much fresh water is flowing in. For example, the Amazon River pumps huge amounts of fresh water, 60 million gallons per

second, into the ocean, so the area around its mouth for 100 miles has less salinity than other areas of the ocean. Water movement also has an impact on the measure of salinity. If the ocean water is moving slowly it generally has a higher salinity than water that is fast-moving.

What Influences the Temperature of Ocean Water?

As you go further and further down into the ocean, the temperature of the water gets colder and colder because it's away from sunlight. Scientists divide the ocean into general layers to describe these temperature changes.

DIVING DEEP INTO THE OCEAN

As you may have suspected, this layer is the warmest. It's the top layer and it gets heated by the sun. The boundary between the surface layer and the thermocline isn't always the same depth and it varies between 100 meters to 300 meters from the surface.

Through the process of convection, the warm ocean water rises. The constant cycle of cooling and heating causes the currents to move within this layer. Depending on the surrounding environment, surface water may be as hot as 30 degrees Celsius near the equator to as cold as about minus 2 degrees Celsius near the poles. The season of the year also impacts the water temperature in the surface zone.

Sea breeze

Land breeze

PROCESS OF CONVECTION

The layer of the ocean under the surface zone is called the thermocline. The temperature decreases as the depth increases. The reason is that the sun's rays can't reach down far enough. Also, the warm water from the layer above doesn't readily mix with the thermocline water. The thermocline's depth varies based on its location. It can extend from 100 meters to nearly 1,000 meters below the ocean's surface.

The layer that goes from the bottom of the thermocline to the bottom of the ocean floor is called the deep zone. The frigid waters of the deep zone are very dense and sluggish, which means that the currents at this depth are very slow. The temperature of the water is an average of about 2 degrees Celsius, which is about 36 degrees Fahrenheit.

The Ocean Floor

Sections of the ocean floor are about 11,000 meters down below the ocean's surface. Human beings cannot survive at that depth without special equipment. First of all, we need to breathe so we can't go down without a way to get oxygen. Secondly, the pressure of the water is so powerful that our bodies couldn't withstand it.

However, this doesn't stop scientists from studying the structure of the ocean depths. There are three ways that they can do it—by using special vehicles, sometimes manned and sometimes unmanned, by using sonar, and by using satellites.

REMOTELY OPERATED
UNDERWATER VEHICLE (ROV)

Features of the Ocean Floor

The floor of the ocean is largely unexplored because of the quantity of salt water that covers it. Just as with the features of Earth's landmasses, many of the features of the ocean floor are created by the Earth's plates, which are massive pieces of rock that float on the Earth's mantle. The movements of these plates is called plate tectonics.

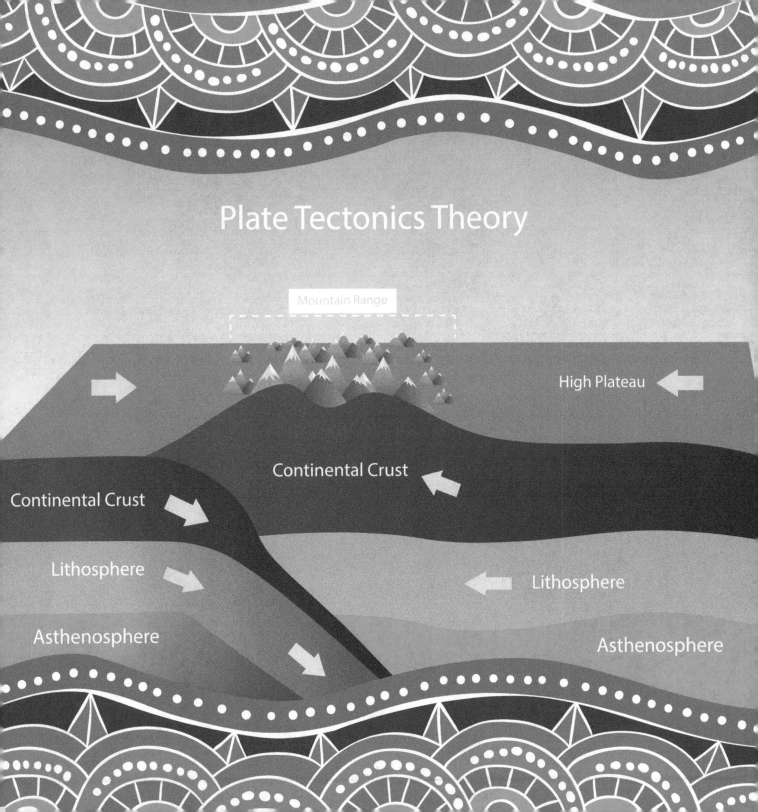

Scientists categorize the ocean's floor into two main regions. One of these regions is known as the continental margin and the other is known as the deep-ocean basin.

The Continental Margin

The continental margin is further divided into three sections. If you were on a beach and you were able to walk down into the ocean, the first section you would come to would be the continental shelf. It starts at the shoreline and gently slopes down. It can reach a depth of about 200 meters.

THE CONTINENTAL MARGIN IS DIVIDED INTO THREE SECTIONS--THE CONTINENTAL SHELF, CONTINENTAL SLOPE, AND CONTINENTAL RISE

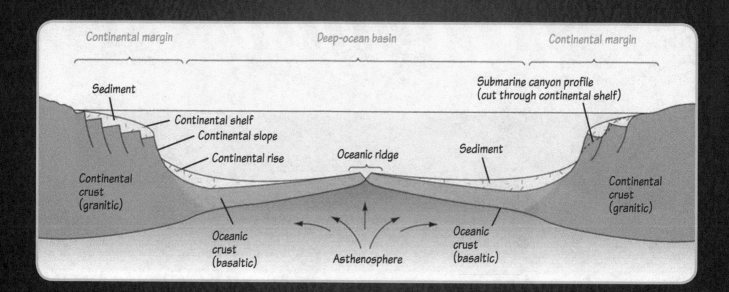

Next, as you continued, would be the continental slope. It's the part of the continental margin that has the steepest slope and continues until it reaches the flattest section of the ocean floor. The continental slope's depth has a range of 200 meters to approximately 4,000 meters. As you continued, you would get to the third section of the continental margin, which is called the continental rise. It is formed by sediment and is at the boundary of the deep-ocean basin.

The Deep Ocean Basin

Next, you would come to the deep-ocean basin. The deep-ocean basin includes many different types of features.

Abyssal plain—an almost level part of the ocean's basin

Mid-ocean ridges—long, underwater ranges of mountains

Rift valleys—narrow valleys formed when tectonic plates move apart

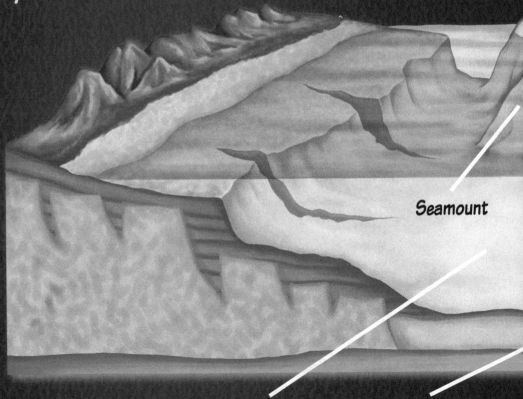

DEEP OCEAN BASIN

Seamount

Abyssal Plain

Mid-Ocean Ridge

Seamount—an underwater mountain at least 1,000 meters in height that was formed by a volcano

Ocean Trenches—steep depressions in the ocean floor caused by the movement of one plate being forced under another

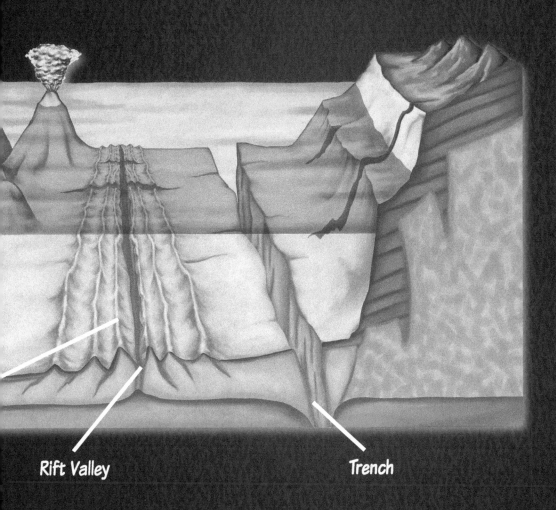

Rift Valley

Trench

Summary

Over 70% of the Earth's surface is covered by a global ocean that can be studied as five different oceans. Our current day oceans were formed by continental drift and the movements of the Earth's plates. The water in the oceans is salt water, which humans can't drink. Fresh water from streams and rivers flows into the ocean, which changes its salinity, the measurement of the dissolved solids in the water. The process of convection causes the water currents to move. Scientists study the features of the ocean floor with special manned and unmanned vehicles that can withstand the immense pressures. They also use sonar and satellites. The ocean floor has features that are similar to the features of landmasses.

Awesome! Now that you've learned about the world's oceans you may want to read about the highest mountains on Earth in the Baby Professor book, The Highest Mountains In The World – Geology for Children | Children's Earth Sciences Books.

9 781541 949676